GEORGE WASHINGTON WILSON
in
CAITHNESS AND SUTHERLAND

Published by Dalesman Publishing Company Ltd., Clapham, Lancaster LA2 8EB
© Aberdeen University Library, 1988
ISBN: 0 85206 950 2
Printed by Fretwell & Cox Ltd., Goulbourne Street, Keighley, West Yorkshire

George Washington Wilson

in

CAITHNESS & SUTHERLAND

John S. Smith
MA. PHD, FSA Scot

Photographs from the George Washington Wilson Collection

Edited for the Library Committee of the University of Aberdeen by
Peter L. Payne

DALESMAN BOOKS
1988

Editor's Preface

George Washington Wilson by Sir George Reid RSA
(reproduced by kind permission of Aberdeen Art Gallery & Museums)

The University of Aberdeen's collection of George Washington Wilson photographic negatives has justifiably been described as a "most valuable storehouse of topographical material." It is more than that: these negatives, which date from c. 1870 to 1908, portray many facets of the infinite variety of late Victorian and Edwardian life not only in Britain but in several places overseas. The collection, consisting of no less than 45,000 glass negatives, comprises what was essentially the stock in trade of George Washington Wilson & Co. when that company went into liquidation in 1908. Started in the early 'fifties by George Washington Wilson, a portrait miniaturist who quickly perceived the commercial potentialities of photography and who pioneered both new methods utilising the wet collodion process (particularly "instantaneous" photography) and remarkably efficient mass production techniques, Wilson combined an artistic sensitivity with great entrepreneurial flair. The firm he created became probably the most important commercial enterprise of its kind in the closing decades of the nineteenth century, enjoying a greater reputation and a larger sale than its principal rivals, the firms established by James Valentine, Francis Firth, William Lawrence and Francis Bedford.

The University's collection has been dipped into to illustrate several important studies in economic and social history and George Washington Wilson himself and the firm that he founded has been the subject of a fascinating monograph by Roger Taylor, George Washington Wilson: Artist and Photographer, 1823–1893 *(Aberdeen University Press, 1981), but the riches of this magnificent collection remain largely unexploited. It is the object of this series of booklets to reveal the great historical and sociological value of the Wilson collection and to provide a fresh viewpoint on the life and landscape of late Victorian Britain and those parts of the world "covered" by the photographers employed by the firm.*

For selecting the photographs of these most northerly parts of the Scottish mainland, and for preparing the text and captions which add so much to our appreciation of these subjects, we are, yet again, indebted to John S. Smith.

Peter L. Payne

Introduction

THE former northern mainland counties of Caithness and Sutherland had much to inspire the Victorian photographer. The scenery offered superb seacliff scapes and mountains, the latter with very considerable potential for postcards in the Scottish 'Bens' series. From vantage points adjacent to the main roads, it was possible even with the rather cumbersome photographic gear of the day, to capture landscapes with an immense depth of field and mountains with extremely distinctive profiles, the latter reflecting their diverse geological composition. Amongst these, Ben Loyal, Ben Arkle and Suilven immediately spring to mind. On the coast, the fretted cliff-girt Caithness coast displayed infinite variations in profile and a number of distinctive sea stacks and caves, their photographic qualities enhanced by Norse names and associations with history and legend. In the remoter parts of the area, the Victorian love of deer sports and river angling had already spawned great lodges and hotels, many of which were to extend their capacity and flex their architectural styles in the last decades of the nineteenth century when the railway provided an easier and more convenient access to at least some parts of these far-flung and remote parts of Britain.

The old historic burghs of Wick and Thurso, while retaining elements of their vernacular cores in buildings and street patterns, both expanded in the middle part of the same century in a planned gridiron arrangement of wide streets, whose frontages were eventually graced by a number of fine new buildings. From the beginning of the nineteenth century, the new fishing town of Pulteneytown, Wick grew rapidly under the aegis of the British Fisheries Society, and retained its position as one of the major centres of the North Sea herring fishery into the present century. In many smaller harbours and creeks along the east Caithness coast, the herring fishery was also being prosecuted with the utmost vigour, the short six-week season being characterised by almost frenzied activity as the highly perishable product was landed, processed and exported to foreign markets. As the plates which follow reveal, the photographer was able to capture in great detail the immense concentration of human energy and financial capital involved — of boats, lines, barrels, curing yards and quayside space. The industry was serviced by a large seasonal influx of workers, many of whom followed the herring fishery around the coast from Shetland to East Anglia. The Victorian photographer's art brings life to the gaunt gridiron streets and quaysides of the contemporary Pulteneytown harbour frontage. At Lybster and Dunbeath, where the landward topography was less favourable than Pulteneytown, every available ledge was taken for curing and storage space, and there must have been considerable strains on accommodation both for boats and people. While investment in harbourage at Wick–Pulteneytown was fairly advanced at the time of George Washington Wilson's visits, at Thurso berthing facilities remained extremely rudimentary in the 1870's and 1880's, with vessels riding out in Scrabster Roads awaiting the spring tides which would permit them to enter the river mouth and lie beached against the quaysides for loading or unloading. Many of Wilson's townscapes of Thurso display the canted masts of schooners beached at the mouth of the Thurso river. Within the town, the gas-lit pavements are well maintained, floored by the flagstone which provided Thurso with one of its major industries and the county with a significant export, while in contrast, the streets remain in generally poor shape, reflecting the legal obligation of shopkeepers to maintain pavement frontages in good repair. A civic acceptance of street surface responsibility apparently postdates the photographer's visits.

The great Caithness castles like Thurso, Dunbeath and Braal also caught the photographer's eye, but in comparison to Orkney and Shetland, there is very limited attention paid to the rural scene other than as incidental parts of plates whose main interest lay in villages or landscape views. Thus the collection of George Washington Wilson photographic plates held by the University of Aberdeen which cover Caithness and Sutherland by no means provides a complete geographical picture or coverage of the area. This may reflect a lack of time, the difficulties of reaching the more inaccessible areas, or Wilson's perception of the market. Alternatively, the surviving plates may not represent the original total stock. Nonetheless, the north-westerly extremity of Cape Wrath was visited on at least one occasion, as views of the lighthouse and nearby cliff scenery attests. From the university's Caithness collection it is possible to determine that a company photographer visited the town of Wick on at least three different occasions. The Station Hotel, Bridge Street, Wick is depicted on three plates, each with a different management — namely Randall's, Ireland's (both incorporating Station Hotel in the title), and the Wick New Hotel. Most of the other plates present difficulties for exact dating, but where approximate dating is possible attention is drawn to this in the captions which accompany the photographs.

The selection that follows may be likened to a photographic journey up the east coast of Sutherland and Caithness, starting at Invershin on the Kyle of Sutherland and ending at Duncansby Head. From Wick and Thurso, the photographic expedition moves westwards along the 'top' to Tongue and Cape Wrath, thence southwards past Ben Arkle, Loch Stack and Culag, Lochinver to Inchnadamph. In Sutherland, the main interest was clearly in landscape photography of the 'hills, glens and bens', while in Caithness, there is little evidence of photographic fieldwork in the interior. Buildings, street scenes, the herring fishery and scenery are the essence of the collection, with rather less emphasis than usual on the human element. Nevertheless, the plates provide a very valuable visual record of Caithness and Sutherland in the 1870's and 1880's, when the primary industries remained the basis of the local economy.

Bibliography

Peter F. Anson, *Fishing Boats and Fisherfolk on the East Coast of Scotland* (London: J.M. Dent and Sons Ltd, 1930).

Jean Dunlop, *The British Fisheries Society 1786–1893* (Edinburgh: John Donald, 1978).

Donald Grant (editor), *Thurso Events* (Thurso: Caithness Books, n.d.).

Donald Grant, *Old Thurso: Caithness Notebook No. 4* (Thurso: Caithness Books, 1966).

New Statistical Account of Scotland, Vol. 15 — Wick parish (Edinburgh, 1845).

Donald Omand (editor), *The Caithness Book* (Inverness: Highland Printers, 1972).

John S. Smith (editor), *The Third Statistical Account of Scotland — The County of Caithness* (Edinburgh: Scottish Academic Press, 1988).

Samuel Smiles, *Robert Dick, Baker of Thurso — Geologist and Botanist* (London: John Murray, 1878).

Robert Louis Stevenson, *Memories and Portraits* (London: 1897).

Thomas Telford, *Survey of the Coasts and Central Highlands* (London: Treasury, 1803).

James Thomson, *The Value and Importance of the Scottish Fisheries* (1849).

Falconer Waters, *Thurso Then and Now* (Thurso: Caithness Books, 1972).

Falconer Waters, *The Story of Thurso Harbour* (Thurso: Caithness Books, n.d.).

Falconer Waters, *Guide to Thurso* (Thurso: Thurso Printers, n.d.).

George Watson, *Caithness Place-Names* (Thurso: Caithness Books, n.d.).

H.A. Vallance, *The Highland Railway* (Newton Abbot, Devon: David and Charles, 1985).

Fishing

THE development of the Caithness herring fisheries led eventually to the construction of harbours and the foundation of new settlements. As early as the 1770's, a fishing station had been established at Staxigoe, although at Wick fishing was carried out from the beach and river mouth, despite the dangers of damage to vessels drawn up on the shore during easterly gales. In 1791, many of the 44 vessels lying in Wick Bay were damaged by storms. Sir John Sinclair, the noted Caithness improver, was in the van of fishing development and, by the end of the eighteenth century, he was pressing for an entirely new settlement and harbour at Wick. By 1803, following favourable reports by the engineers John Rennie and Thomas Telford, land was purchased by the British Fisheries Society on the southern side of the Wick River, and a start made to the feuing of Pulteneytown. An inner harbour was begun in 1807 and completed in 1811. The bounty system of subsidies which had been introduced in 1750 was extended in 1797 and again in 1815. Dutch expertise was applied to improvement in curing methods, particularly essential in remote areas distant from markets.

At the smaller creeks — essentially goe-heads on a cliff-girt coastline — villages were built on the clifftop, the often very restricted goe-head shore ledges being reserved for quay space and ground for storage and curing operations. One of the earliest of these planned fishing villages was Sarclet, which was laid out four miles south of Wick in 1788. Still earlier, fisheries had been established at Dunbeath and Clyth; while at Lybster, Sinclair was responsible for the construction of the first pier in 1810. Further improvements were made at Lybster in the 1830's. These provided a basin which could accommodate 120 undecked fishing boats and sufficient depth to enable the 100-ton vessels, which brought in the barrel staves and salt and took out the cured herring for export, to be berthed in comparative safety. Additional harbour improvements were carried out at Lybster in the 1850's.

In contrast to Pulteneytown, where the British Fisheries Society aimed at establishing a settlement 'crewed' by professional fishermen and service occupations, most of the other Caithness and Sutherland fishing settlements were peopled by crofters looking to the herring season as a means of supplementing their agricultural income. The population of the eastern seaboard parishes, notably Latheron, was swollen by families from Sutherland moved from their ground as a result of the Clearances and seeking homes and employment. In addition, local crews were augmented by seasonal immigrants from the Western Isles, usually engaged on a share-of-catch basis.

During the season, which started in July, every available space was utilised on the shorehead. The landing, gutting, curing and packing, and the storage of barrels, placed considerable demands on sites which were frequently extremely constricted. With a highly perishable commodity like herring, the speed of preparation determined the quality of the final product. The scenes of Pulteneytown and Lybster all display an orderly layout of working areas and materials.

By the time the photographs which illustrate this booklet were taken, the herring fisheries had already peaked in Caithness, at least in terms of numbers employed and boats operating. The small undecked fishing boats of approximately 10-tons — the Fifies and Zulus — were already being modified and replaced by larger wholly or partially decked boats, often with a hand-winch fitted to reduce the immense labour involved in hauling the nets. As the boats became bigger and their individual catching power increased, the number of landing points contracted to the larger harbours — a trend to be accelerated by the introduction of the steam drifter around the end of the nineteenth century. By then, herring fishing had become an all-year-round occupation manned entirely by professional fishermen.

The Fishing season at Wick — boats sailing. Scaffies leaving the harbour mouth at Wick and eventually catching the wind. Within the harbour, as seen in a later plate, congestion made movement into open water extremely difficult. A North Company boat lies anchored in inner Wick Bay. The scaffie with sail drawing carries a crew of five.

Wick Harbour — the herring season. Much 'poling' is going on here at the exit from the outer harbour, with boats preparing to leave *en masse* for the fishing grounds in the late afternoon. Harbour Terrace is visible in the background, with the roofs of Breadalbane Terrace beyond. A sign in the former street advertises 'Rope and Sail'. The overnight fishing was followed by a frantic dash to harbour to land the highly perishable commodity. Writing in 1849, James Thomson wrote of Wick Harbour that it 'presents a spectacle in the months of July and August of a peculiar kind, not to be met with in this part of the world, if indeed, in any other. From the heights of Pulteneytown, overlooking the quays and curer's stations, one has before him, as it were, an extended plain, covered with thousands and tens of thousands of barrels, interspersed at short distances with the busy scene of delivery, of packing and of salting, and all the bustle and detail attendant on the cure' (*Scottish Fisheries,* 1849). Fortunately, the photographs cannot convey what the minister of the *New Statistical Account* termed 'a putrescent effluvia steaming up from the fish offals'.

Wick Harbour: the 'stump' of the Stevenson breakwater, which was destroyed by a storm in 1872. This breakwater, which cost the British Fisheries Society today's equivalent of £10m, was under construction in the period 1863–1870. As early as 1858, a Royal Commission had recognised the advantages of Wick Bay and recommended the building of a breakwater, but no money was forthcoming from the Government. The pressure on the Society to take independent action mounted over the years. Between 1845 and 1863, about 150 fishermen had been drowned and over 400 boats wrecked in the vicinity of Wick, while the activities of the Society (and the interests of its Directors) became increasingly concentrated in Pulteneytown. Thus, despite continual storm damage, the Society pressed on with breakwater construction, although the work was on a scale more appropriate to that undertaken by the national government. During this period, stone was transported from the South Head quarries using bogies drawn by a miniature locomotive. Robert Louis Stevenson, author and son of one of the consulting engineers, Messrs D. and T. Stevenson of Edinburgh, described Wick harbour as 'the chief disaster of my father's life . . . the sea proved too strong for man's arts; and after expeditions hitherto unthought of, and on a scale hypercyclopean, the work must be deserted and now stands a ruin in that God-forsaken bay, ten miles from John-O'-Groats' (*Memories and Portraits*, 1887). In the future, all harbour works on this scale were to be funded by the state. In the photograph, a small lodberry sits immediately upriver of the breakwater; the 120 scaffies lying offshore indicate the pressure on the harbour.

Herring Season at Wick — a fair catch. The old style undecked boats continued to be used in the '70's and '80's, despite dangers to their crew during heavy weather. The view clearly illustrates the advantages for catch storage space, although it left the minimum of room for crew and fishing gear.

An August scene in the Outer Harbour, Wick, with the Customs House and Steamer Office in the left background. The apparatus of curing, which remained an essentially outdoor occupation, dominates the landward scene. The old links or backlands along the southern margin of Wick Bay provided 'the extended plain' described by James Thomson in 1849. The empty farlins in the middle foreground contrast with the frenzied activity on the quay where the figures are blurred because of the long exposure. Following gutting, the herring catch was packed in salt in the barrels, which lay open for around a week to ten days awaiting final inspection and closure. As the herring required gutting, curing and packing within at least 24 hours of landing (and landings were on a daily basis), it was essential to accumulate the necessary raw materials — barrels and salt — in advance for speedy and efficient preparation.

Pulteneytown Harbour, Wick. The planned fishery settlement of Pulteneytown was named after a director of the British Fisheries Society, Sir William Pulteney. The Society, founded in 1786, resulted from the desire, shared by both a Parliamentary Committee on the Fisheries and the Highland Society of London, to stimulate development in the Highlands of Scotland. In the important formative period, when suitable sites were being surveyed, John Mackenzie of Tarradale was secretary of both Societies. Although the British Fisheries Society had initially investigated the north and western coasts of the Highlands, Thomas Telford was requested to report on the coast from Duncansby Head to Portmahomack. His recommendation in 1790 was that the Society consider the improvement of the natural harbour at Wick, where a small fishery was already operating, despite difficulties from lack of harbour works. The *Old Statistical Account* of 1793 indicated that Wick's population of around 1000 included 50 coopers and about ten shipmasters. The momentum for investing in Wick was increased by the appointment of Sir John Sinclair as a director of the Society in 1792. Both north and south banks of Wick Bay were owned by Sir Benjamin Dunbar of Hempriggs, who had himself established a small fishing station at Louisburgh, just north of Wick.

In 1803, a contract between the Society and Sir Benjamin Dunbar brought just under 400 acres on the south side of the river under their control, providing backlands for the new town layout, the waterfront, and potential quarry sites for building stone. The main section of the new town was almost completed within twenty years, with the lower ground adjoining the river divided up into standard lots for curing houses and ancillary services. On the north bank, various small harbourages and short jetties were constructed by private enterprise. By 1830, Pulteneytown had a resident population of around 2,200, with the storehouses and curing houses on the shore ledge and the residential areas on the higher ground behind. During the summer herring season, the town's population increased by a further 7000.

The photograph shows the outer harbour with entrance lighthouse, the former designed by Telford and completed by 1834. The scene is dominated by Wick-registered 'scaffies', although one Stornoway boat is present. The farlins are mainly empty but women are busy at the water's edge washing out the contents (possibly offal) of small tubs. Schooners in the inner harbour and along the North pier are lined up ready to load herring barrels; they are riding high out the water. The total scene suggests a general tidying up for the weekend. Further curing stations at Willowbank and Hillhead (Port Dunbar) are visible on the north bank. Towards the end of the century, export of herring was carried out largely by steam-powered vessels, suggesting this scene dates from the 1880's.

This view, which pans east from the previous one, concentrates on the Outer Harbour of Pulteneytown, with teams of gutters and packers in action. In a scene dominated by the masts of the sail boats, several small schooners, including the 'Jewess', are being loaded with barrels. The quayside, which is much encumbered with guts and salt, shows the tracks of countless carts removing the offal and barrel carts for loading the schooners. Further swarms of sail vessels are moored off the curing yards of Shaltiegoe.

A peaceful early morning view of Helmsdale from the old castle, the ruins of which were to be totally removed by the construction of a new road bridge in 1972. The village was planned under the aegis of the Duke of Sutherland as a part of the major changes in estate management and land use policy undertaken during the early 19th century. Houses and curing sheds alike are planned and executed to high standards. The three boats with sails hoisted carry nets and floats on deck, but there is no sign onshore of preparation for the morning landings. This suggests that the photographers' visit coincided with the end of the season at a period in the herring fishery when activities were heavily concentrated at Wick. The trim, white-washed houses on Dunrobin Street appear to have substantial gardens, some of which are well-tended. In contrast to the Sutherland Estates, the British Fishery Society policy in Pulteneytown strictly specified no gardens, mainly because of the likely build-up of the inevitable and unhygienic midden. Furthermore, at Pulteneytown the Society wished to create a group of professional fishermen in contrast to crofter-fishermen. The suspicion that the boats are merely drying sails is confirmed by the following view looking upriver, where the sealed barrels are stacked horizontally for export by sea. The church and school are prominent in the middle background, with bank and post office to the right at the lower end of Lichfield Street (later re-named Station Street).

The United Free church and manse and the Commercial Hotel are prominent in this view looking up the Helmsdale valley. In the background are the thatched croft houses of Old Helmsdale, Almshouses and Carnlaggie, the crofting strips of West Helmsdale and the line of the railway (1871). In 1845, in his *Report on the State of the Harbours of Scotland*, the Examining Commissioner drew attention to the great want of space for the 220 boats which frequented Helmsdale during the season, but James Thomson in *Scottish Fisheries* (1849), while also lamenting the small size of the harbour, noted that the 'curing stations are about the most complete on the coast ... fitted up on the most convenient plan, roomy, substantial and having every necessary appendage in store houses, packing sheds and salt cellars'. The inference is that at Helmsdale a fair amount of the onerous work of curing and packing took place indoors. This may have been one of the factors behind the high reputation which the Helmsdale product enjoyed in the middle years of the nineteenth century.

This view of Lybster village and harbour from the south east predates the completion of the Duke of Portland's major improvements to the harbour, including the pierhead lighthouse (1884). A pier constructed at the burn outlet by Sinclair in 1810 was followed by the development of a harbour in 1832. This early harbour (featured in the following photograph) could berth the 100-ton vessels used for the import of salt and staves and the export of the cured herring. By 1849, the size of the fishing fleet during the season was such that the harbour could not accommodate the landings. Nonetheless, some 20,000 barrels were cured at Lybster in 1883. In that year the Duke of Portland commenced a five-year programme of harbour improvements and extensions to the curing areas, but by 1895, only 50 boats were landing here in comparison with a total of 300 in the early '80's. With the development of steam drifters, many Lybster fishermen moved to Wick.

Lybster harbour after the completion of the Duke of Portland's improvements to the harbour and the curing space. The premium on space for curing and storage of barrels is apparent. In the basin, small schooners await cargo of cured herring, while in the right background the small boat building yard continues to operate.

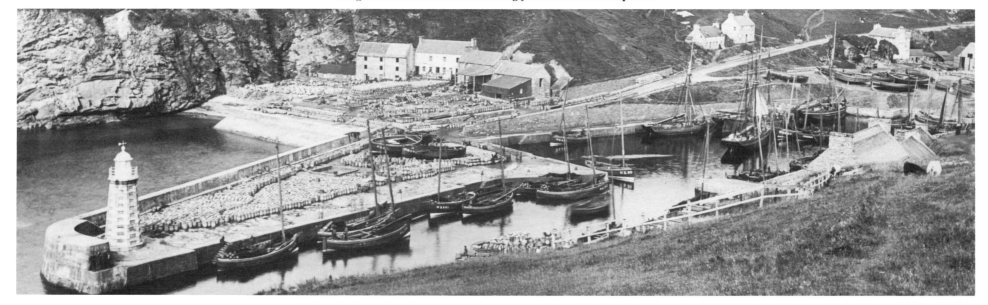

A general view of Scrabster, illustrating (from left to right) the post office, lifeboat station (gable-end to shore, now Rose Cottage), Custom House, hotel, chapel, and (landward of the small schooner) the flagstone works, and beyond, a warehouse. A Northern Isles steamer and small paddle steamer are moored at the pier, with the lighthouse in the background. Land reclamation and quay construction are ongoing in the left foreground. The first regular mail-service between Scrabster and Stromness began in 1865. The paddle steamer *Royal Mail* operated by the Highland Railway Company took over in 1877, and in 1882 the North of Scotland Steam navigation Co. Ltd. began operating the *St. Olaf*, which ran until 1892. It is almost certain that the steamer moored at the pier is the *St. Olaf*.

On Scrabster quay, farlins, barrels and barrel lids are stored, with a team of women completing the packing before each barrel is inspected and sealed. The farlins on the left are empty. A sea of masts on the other side of the pier represent the fleet, while on the extreme left a small steamer is loading herring barrels. The profusion of barrel storage visible in this picture contrasts with the previous photograph of Scrabster where the same space is unoccupied save by a single sheerlegs.

Wick

WICK, like Thurso, takes its name from Norse orgins, the word meaning a bay. This became transferred to the settlement which grew up at the southern end of Sinclair's Bay. Although a site of historical importance, and a settlement which, like Thurso, exported boiled and pickled salmon, salted and cured herring in the 1760's, real growth in and around Wick dates from the latter part of the 18th century when the Caithness herring fishery began to expand. In a survey of the *Coasts and Central Highlands of Scotland* presented to the Lord Commissioners of His Majesty's Treasury in 1803, Thomas Telford, although mainly concerned with the Caledonian Canal, mentions possible naval stations, and 'The Emigrations' includes as *Appendix 8* a report on Wick, dated 1801. Telford draws attention to the fact that while on the west coast 'every loch is a harbour', there was then nowhere on the east coast from Cromarty to the roadstead of Scrabster where 'a vessel can run into or even lie with safety'. Because of the inconvenience, danger and damage to the highly perishable commodity of herring caused by delay and by berthing on the beach, he recommends that 'there should be a harbour on the coast of Caithness; and there is no place, except Wick, to the south of the Pentland Firth, which is fit for such a harbour' (Telford, 1803). In making this assessment of Wick's potential for harbour construction, Telford was re-iterating John Rennie's report of 1793 made to the Directors of the British Fisheries Society. This commends Wick to the Society as 'a proper station for the fisher'. Rennie also notes that 'the town of Wick contains several hundred inhabitants, has a church and a school'. The need for harbourage to promote the fisheries was reinforced by the experience of August, 1792 when despite the presence at Wick of some 30 fishing vessels, the necessity to beach them at spring tide for safety reasons shoreward of the Wick river mouth submarine sand bar, meant that, on the arrival of a herring shoal, few vessels could get to sea for catching operations. As indicated above, the Society eventually invested in 400 acres of land on the southern side of the river from Old Wick, and constructed the new town of Pulteneytown, in part from a grant derived from the income of the Forfeited Estates. Initially a harbour to accommodate 100 fishing vessels was built with associated shore support, notably curing sheds, and this harbour was enlarged in 1824. Further projected improvements included the construction of a breakwater which was begun in 1863, virtually destroyed by a great storm in 1868, and finally abandoned in 1872. At that time the breakwater had cost the Society some £150,000. In 1879, control of the harbour was transferred from the Society to a Board of Harbour Trustees. By 1795, there were 200 open boats fishing from Wick during the season, and by 1840, in excess of 750, with over 3800 fishermen in the town. The curers of Pulteneytown employed around 2000 gutters, and there were 265 coopers in employment. During the season there was a vast influx of seasonal labour into Pulteneytown, many from the Western mainland and from Lewis. The *New Statistical Account* for Wick parish (1840) draws attention to the social problems caused by the seasonal influx of several thousands of 'strangers' into a town whose main facility for entertainment consisted of the 45 public houses then in existence in Wick and Pulteneytown. In the year 1862, 1122 boats fished from Wick during the herring season, and while the numbers operating during Wilson's visit in the last decades of the 19th century were apparently much lower, the harbour scenes eloquently convey the great activity of the season, set against the rather drab austerity of Pulteneytown's flagstone buildings. While one can understand the *cri de coeur* of the minister writing in 1840 that 'no care was taken of the 10,000 young strangers of both sexes who were crowded together with the inhabitants within the narrow limits of Wick during the six principal weeks of the fishing, exposed to drink and numerous other temptations' (*New Statistical Account*, 1840), one can sympathise with their behaviour. In the same year, The Wick and Pulteneytown Total Abstinence Society was founded. It soon attracted a membership of 700! Overcrowding in Pulteneytown was a continual problem. As late as 1884, only nine years before the British Fisheries Society was wound up, the Directors were reporting that several new streets had been 'laid out' to relieve the overcrowding in existing houses, but by then the herring fishery was passing through a depression from which it never really recovered, although some of the lost ground in continental markets was regained through more attention being paid to the quality of the product.

In terms of 19th century population growth, the upstart Pulteneytown quickly dwarfed Wick, the royal burgh. The combined totals grew from 1,749 in 1811, to 5,522 in 1840, and to 8,053 in 1881. Although the combined population continued to grow until a maximum of 8,674 was reached in 1911, the slump of the early 1880's virtually halted building in Pulteneytown. some of the apparently unfinished, untenanted buildings caught in the photographer's lens may reflect this period of difficulty.

The view of Pulteneytown from the Ramsgoe area looks across a forest of masts. The generally level horizon of Pulteneytown is punctuated by chimneys and, to the right, the spire of the Old Parish Church is prominent across the Wick River. Shore stabilisation work is ongoing to the east of the Outer Harbour (the lighthouse is shown slightly left of centre), while the Inner Harbour contains masted schooners, presumably loading herring barrels. The relative size of the Pulteneytown development (by contrast with the old town of Wick) is clearly apparent. Until the very end of the 19th century, the affairs of Pulteneytown were administered by Commissioners, while those of the burgh were run by the Town Council. In the middle years of the century there was considerable rivalry between the two settlements.

Wick Old Parish Church and Manse (to left), with the first mansions of Miller Avenue (then Miller Street) apparent. The weir on the Wick river permitted boating during the summer months.

A view of the western end of the High Street with white-washed, crow-stepped gabled cottages contrasting with the more recent squat flagstone houses. The Town Hall and Bridge Street Church are prominent at the northern end of the new bridge, and Pulteneytown may be glimpsed in the distant horizon. The distinctive cemetery of Wick Old Parish church is in the immediate foreground.

Bridge Street, Wick, with Randall's Station Hotel, the Commercial Bank, Church of Scotland and the Town Hall.

The New Bridge, with Ireland's Station Hotel, the spire of the Free Church (now Church of Scotland), and the Drill Hall on far left. The chimney of Wick Steam Mills (saw and corn mill) protrudes above the roofs on the extreme right, while the masts of schooners break the skyline in the middle distance.

The riverside frontages of Wick below the new bridge, with much evidence of saw mill activity and timber storage.

Thurso

THE distinguished historical pedigree of Thurso has been delightfully sketched by Donald Grant in his *Old Thurso* (1966). Evidence of its Norse origins are clear from frequent mentions in the Old Norse Sagas, but opinions differ over the real meaning of its name. Perhaps the most likely derivation is *Thor's haugr* — Thor's mound — although it cannot be determined with certainty whether the mound commemorated is a Norse burial place or the site of the old Norse castle at Ormlie. By the 18th century, Thurso was clustered compactly around the High Street, Bank Street and Shore Street. A small fishertown stood at the river mouth where boats and small trading vessels could be beached. The old tolbooth at the corner of Bank Street was already in ruins by the 1760's and the affairs of the free burgh of barony were conducted from the session-house of Old St. Peter's Church, with the vault below serving as a temporary prison. The market was held on open ground in the vicinity of the present Town Hall (1871).

Thurso began to expand beyond its medieval bounds during and after the last few decades of the 18th century, when Sir John Sinclair began the planned developments to the south of Olrig Street. These remarkably *avant-garde* plans were eventually to lead to the feuing of the new thoroughfares of Princes Street and Traill Street. Sir John and his successors were able to play major roles in Thurso's early town planning because historically they held the right of superiorship, and thus were entitled to appoint baillies and councillors as well as town officials. Only in the second half of the 19th century did Thurso obtain Parliamentary sanction to hold free and binding burgh elections, where elected representatives could no longer be vetoed by the superior. Nevertheless, the Sinclair family retained a continuing influence on Thurso's development, notably through gifts of land.

The development of adequate harbourage at the mouth of the Thurso river was a long drawn-out affair. Despite the absence of a harbour, Thurso exported meal, beef, skins and hides throughout the 18th century, although, unlike Wick, these goods were carried by shipping from other ports. There was considerably rivalry with Wick, but Thurso retained the advantage because at the time of the Act of union in 1701 it was declared a legalised port with Custom's Office and a designed area of monopoly. As early as 1802, again largely under the aegis of Sir John Sinclair, an Act of Parliament was passed authorising the construction of an ambitious harbour at Thurso, incorporating a graving dock and shipbuilding slip. The proposal failed for lack of money. By 1825, however, Thurso boasted 17 ships with a total gross tonnage of 1,035 tons, and had already appointed a Shoremaster to manage the beaching of vessels along the riverside. The development of the nearby sandstone quarries for paving stones encouraged the establishment of cutting and polishing yards along both banks of the Thurso river. This lead eventually to problems of encroachment by these yards on land earmarked for future harbour improvements, and to the utilisation of space already employed by the fishing community at Fisherbiggins. Only during the 1890's was work set in hand under the Thurso River Harbour Bill of 1889, but few of the proposals contained in the original scheme were ever satisfactorily completed.

Despite an extension of the breakwater, the entrance channel remained shallow and narrow, and schooners trading to Thurso, or seeking cargos of paving stones had, in George Washington Wilson's day, to enter at spring tides. This could be accomplished only under certain wind directions and with the assistance of hauling by ropes using casual labour. Vessels frequently awaited favourable tide and wind circumstances by mooring in Scrabster Bay. Once berthed within the river, the boats took the ground during the lower states of the tide and, in many cases, were loaded by carts operating at low tide. The tilted masts on Wilson's photographs clearly illustrate the problems of berthage.

The New Town planned by Sir John is centred on Sir John Square and is laid out on a rectlinear plan. The first bridge across the Thurso river was opened in 1800 and replaced in 1887. Improved land communications with the south commenced in 1816, with the first regular mail coach service, while the railway station on the periphery of the New Town was opened in 1874. Although Thurso was historically the main seaport for Caithness, the construction of the Pulteneytown harbour across the river from its arch-rival Wick in 1808 effectively eroded that position, although Thurso retained dominance in the export of paving stones. As the century progressed, Wick's population growth greatly exceeded that of Thurso. In 1840, the steamers of the Orkney and Shetland Steam navigation Company began a regular service between Wick and Aberdeen. However, Thurso's maritime connections were ensured by the development of nearby Scrabster as the port for the Orkneys.

In more recent times, the construction and operation of the Atomic Energy Establishment at Dounreay has been responsible for a major increase in housing and services at Thurso. Between 1951 and 1961, Thurso's population increased from 3,224 to 8,276. Strict conservation measures and enlightened urban renewal schemes within Thurso have, however, ensured that both the historic core areas around St. Peter's Church, Shore Street and High Street, and the older houses of Sir John's New Town have retained much of the character they had in George Washington Wilson's day.

The Established Church (St. Peter's Church), Thurso, was opened in 1833 to replace the near ruinous Old St. Peter's Kirk. The area in front of the church was presented to Thurso by Sir Tollemache Sinclair in 1879 with the intention that it should be an enclosed garden. In 1893, with the erection of the statue of Sir John Sinclair, the great Caithness agricultural improver, and Sir Tollemache's grandfather, the area became known as Sir John Square. The photograph appears to pre-date the construction of the Temperance Hotel. Although the town clock shows thirty-five minutes past one, the group of children lining the railings and church entrance strongly suggests recent release from Sunday School. The gridiron pattern junctions of Barrock and Rose Streets are emphasised by the rows of gables to the left of the church.

The Academy, Thurso. The Miller Academy was opened in 1862 as a school for boys and named after its benefactor, Mr. Alexander Miller. When opened, its teachers offered English, Mathematics, Latin, Greek and French at the going rate of £0.33½d per quarter session. Under the provision of the 1872 Education Act, all schools (whether parochial or General Assembly) were transferred to elected Parish School Boards. The building is now the library of the Miller Institution. As the plaque above the entrance indicates, it was originally known as the Miller Institution. This fine squat classical building stands at the west end of Sinclair Street.

This view along Traill Street looks towards the Miller Institution (far distance). The well-maintained flagstone pavements and gutters contrast with the high-cambered 'dirt' road surface. In those days, the maintenance of footpaths was the responsibility of the proprietors. The spire of the West Church is visible in the middle distance. The street is named after James Traill of Rattar who pioneered the Castletown flagstone industry. The Druggist (Bremners) on the immediate left is now the Ship's Wheel, while just beyond (behind the wall and railings) is Manson's Lane, the site of the Meadow Well, Thurso's original water supply, and one of the most popular meeting places in the old days.

A later view of Triall Street shows the frontage of the Meadow Well site, now built on and occupied by Andersons, locksmiths (key-maker sign on left middle distance). The work of the photographer, with the necessary long exposures, has clearly excited interest amongst the bystanders and some at least of those in the immediate foreground have been persuaded to 'freeze'. The *Pictorial Post* is advertised at the newsagents in the right foreground and a selection of postcards is displayed. To judge by the number of names and window frontages, Triall street is already becoming an important shopping street. Gas lighting (introduced to the burgh in 1846) is very much in evidence.

Thurso's Esplanade (defined as any level space for walking or driving on), was built in 1882, using funds raised by public subscription. It also provided a welcome shore defence line against progressive inroads into the Links of Ormlie made during high seas. The view looks eastwards past the old Salvation Army Hall (1799), with the clustered ranks of the fisher quarter on the right distance (Fisher Biggings). Beyond the river mouth, Thurso Castle (1872) is prominent in its late Victorian splendour. In 1894, the Town Commissioners of Thurso laid down regulations for public bathing off the Esplanade. These chiefly involved the delimitation of segregated bathing areas for ladies and gentlemen, the prohibition of dumping of rubbish on the sea beach, and the prohibition of the washing and exercising of dogs and horses within the defined bathing areas between 8am and 6pm during the summer months. It was specified that male bathers exercising after 8am had to wear bathing costumes.

Thurso Town Hall (1871) stands at the south western end of the old High Street (once the site of the gallows and market cross), the centre of the old town's commercial life, with its weekly market. The site of William Bremner's shop is now occupied by Woolworth's and the square has been pedestrianised. The firmly-shuttered building to the right of the Town Hall appears to be unoccupied.

A view of Princes Street, Thurso, taken from just north of the Temperance Hotel whose sign is visible beside the group of bystanders. The hotel occupied the upper level of the Cooperative Building. Sir John's Square and St. Peter's Church, both surrounded by railings, are just visible to left and right respectively. The name, Princes Street, commemorates a visit to Thurso in 1876 of the Prince and Princess of Wales to open an exhibition of Art and Industry. The cart in the right foreground is making a mid-morning delivery — including loaves (from the St. Clair Bakery?) and crates of liquid refreshment — to the Cooperative.

The mansions of Janet Street were among the earliest parts of the 19th century New Town of Thurso to be developed. The street took its name from Sir John Sinclair's mother, and was enhanced in 1894 by the gift of the riverine strip of land from Sir Tollemache Sinclair. The pleasant linear area became known as "The Mall", after a combination of town money and public subscription had created an attractive parkland atmosphere. The photograph highlights the bridge across the Thurso river (1887), the chimneys of pavement works on the east side of the river, the Thurso Castle (1872). The walled lane on the immediate left is the old entrance to the Miller Institution.

The photograph looks towards the Fisherbiggins, the chimney of the Braehead Pavement Works and the Thurso Pavement Works, the latter on the eastern side of the river. The unsatisfactory nature of the tidal wharfage at the river mouth is clearly demonstrated. By the middle of the 19th century, most of the useful riverbank space had been developed by pavement merchants. Their technique was to construct walls along the bank and then infill with tailings from their cutting yards. In the absence of a proper harbour, the vessels, chiefly schooners, entered the river mouth during spring tides and were beached for loading or unloading. Those awaiting a favourable tide to enter generally anchored in Scrabster roads. As the century progressed the original breakwater of 1855 became increasingly ruinous. Only in the 1870's was a concerted attempt made to assert a measure of control over bank development through the formation of a Harbour Trust. In 1889, the Thurso River Harbour Bill became law and work on implementing its provisions commenced in 1891. The schooners beached on both banks brought in coal, timber and salt, and exported paving stones. Because of the narrowness of the pre-improvement entrance channel, vessels were often hauled in using casual labour. The dumping of paving debris from the yards is clearly visible on the east bank of the river. The stepping stones, which are shown in an 1878 photograph of the Thurso River mouth in Falconer Water's booklet on *Thurso Harbour*, provided a convenient shortcut for those flagstone workers engaged on the east bank of the river. This photograph appears to pre-date the reconstruction of Thurso Castle in 1872.

This view of Thurso from Oldfield Farm highlights St. Peter's (1832), the West Church on Sinclair Street, and the Episcopal Church (1885) without its chancel (added 1906). The old bridge (1800–1887) with its toll house is also visible. Cloth bleaching is evident along the strip later known as "The Mall".

Landscapes

Loch Culag, Lochinver, with the schoolhouse in the background.

Aultnagalagach Lodge, Sutherland, with Suilven in the background.

Kinloch Lodge and Ben Hope at the head of the Kyle of Tongue, Sutherland.

Berriedale Glen, Caithness, with the Scarabens in the background.

Inchnadamph and Ben More Assynt, Sutherland.

Rocks

MOST of the rocks outcropping along the Caithness coast are of the Middle Old Red Sandstone group. Originally these were deposited as the debris derived from weathering of the primeval Scottish land surface and laid down by streams in valleys, lakes and mountain basins. Although these fresh water bodies were often extensive, during droughts evaporation reduced them to small pools of water, separated by dried-up sandflats. Although the main area of sedimentation bordered what is now the Moray Firth, small outliers of the Old Red near Tongue in Sutherland strongly suggest an originally much more widespread sandstone cover. Once compacted by the sheer weight of sediment accumulation into sandstone, the layers were subsequently faulted and folded by neighbouring mountain-building episodes, and joint systems developed as a result of stress relaxation, frequently running at high angles to the main bedding layers. These joints, small faults and the angles of the bedding layers (known as the dip) determine the weaknesses later exploited by weathering and wave processes, particularly along cliffy coasts, and are responsible for its architectural characteristics.

The often subtle changes in composition within the Old Red Sandstone sequence, coupled with the differing joint densities, have created intricate variations in cliff plan and profile which have attracted traveller and photographer alike. Very impressive tabular cliff, goe (inlet) and stack scenery occurs, especially where, as at Duncansby, near horizontally-bedded or gently dipping sandstone beds are attacked by marine activities funnelled along near vertical master joints.

In Sutherland, west of the Moine thrust, particularly in the vicinity of this immense geological dislocation, beds of older rocks, often of widely differing ages and characteristics have been sandwiched together to produce mountains with high distinctive profiles such as Arkle. In addition, a narrow belt of limestones, notably outcropping in the classic geologist's territory of Assynt, has created opportunities for solution to produce disappearing streams and underground caves as at Inchnadamph. Thus geology and scenery provided the opportunity for George Washington Wilson's team to produce early versions of what are currently classic viewpoints for photographers.

The Stacks of Duncansbay, Caithness.

The role of the vertical joints in providing zones of weakness for wave attack and weathering disintegration is well displayed in this view of the Tinker's Cave, near Wick. As with many such caves in late nineteenth century North Britain, periodic summer occupation by travelling people was commonplace.

The often tabular, 'lego'-like characteristics of the Caithness coast is evident in this view of the Clett Rock, Thurso.

This view features the shooting lodge by Loch Stack, with the fine geological sandwich of Ben Arkle in the background. The line of screes running diagonally upwards from right to left marks the junction between the underlying Lewisian gneiss and the thrust Cambrian quartzites.

This view, entitled by Wilson 'the spillwater of the underground river, Inchnadamph', illustrates the general absence of surface drainage — except during spates — in this limestone country closely associated with the Moine Thrust.

Castles

Although the site of Thurso Castle has been occupied by a fortified building since the 17th century, when it was a stronghold of the Earls of Caithness, the building featured in this photograph dates from 1872. In that year, Thurso's benefactor Sir Tollemache Sinclair demolished the existing building and rebuilt in chateau-style. Its crenulations and turrets seem to have been associated with a desire to display a certain flamboyance. The flags on the schooners at the river mouth and the bedecked castle strongly suggest that the photographer was present on the day in 1876 when Sir Tollemache entertained the Prince and Princess of Wales to lunch. The *Thurso Tatler* of 3rd October, 1876, estimated that a crowd of 'fully 12,000' had been present in Thurso on the previous day, when the Prince and Princess of Wales formally opened the Exhibition of Fine Art and Industry held in the old Free Church. Shortly afterwards, the Commissioners agreed to change the name of the thoroughfare of Ulbster Terrace, Forss Street and Sutherland Street to Princes Street, as a permanent reminder of the occasion. In the 1950's, the upper parts of Thurso Castle were demolished for safety reasons.

The original 17th century house of Dunbeath was built on a clifftop promontory with a landward dry ditch. It is likely that masonry from at least as early as the 15th century lies below. The name Dunbeath also appears as the site of a battle during the Dark Ages. The 17th century house was a four-storeyed oblong structure, but it has been substantially modified and added to in more modern times, in particular on its eastern side. The older structure remains in part within the modern castle. The last major reconstructions were completed in 1881.

Girnigoe Castle stands on a promontory facing Sinclair's Bay. The landward egress was guarded by a pair of dry ditches. Like Thurso Castle, it was originally a stronghold of the Earls of Caithness, dating from the end of the 15th century when William, 2nd Earl of Caithness, commenced construction. By the beginning of the 18th century the castle, probably already ruinous, had passed to the Sinclairs. The last additions date from the 5th Earl of Caithness in the 1670's, but much of what stands erect in the photograph appears to date from the 15th century. As can be seen, the thinly laminated sandstone beds of the promontory form a secure base for the oblong tower.

Ackergill is basically a 15th century tower of five storeys, the fifth of which was rebuilt in the 19th century. Other modern additions include a wing and considerable modification of the fenestration. Families associated with its history include the Cheynes, the Keith Marischals, the Oliphants and the Dunbars of Hempriggs.

The superb Inverary-style frontage of Thurso Castle as it was towards the end of the 19th century, following Sir Tollemache Sinclair's reconstruction.

Braal Castle, near Halkirk, Caithness.

The Bishop's Castle, Thurso, often known historically as Scrabster Castle, sits at the eastern end of the Braes of Scrabster overlooking Thurso Bay. It was one of the residences of the early Caithness bishops, some of whom may have required protection from the local inhabitants or, indeed, from their neighbours across the Firth in Orkney. The mound of debris featured in the photograph, with masonry of the remains of a tower protruding at the back, is probably the place where Earl Harald of Orkney mutilated Bishop John, c.1196, the site then being known as 'the borg at Skarabolstad'. Excavations in the 1970's revealed something of the form of the buildings and provided evidence of their continued occupation during the medieval period.

Pictish Tower, Dunrobin. This view of Carn Liath broch, Golspie, Sutherland, post-dates the excavations carried out by the Third Duke of Sutherland in 1871. The excavation largely took the form of emptying out the fallen debris from its interior.

Dunrobin Castle is alleged to be one of the oldest inhabited buildings in Scotland. Parts of the fabric are believed to have built by Robert, Earl of Sutherland, in 1098. The present building largely dates from major renovations and extensions carried out in the late 1840's.

Railways

THE railway from Bonar Bridge to Golspie was completed by the Sutherland Railway Company in 1868. The 17 miles of line from Golspie to Helmsdale was built at his own expense by the 3rd Duke of Sutherland at a cost of just over £70,000. In 1884, the Duke sold out his undertaking to the Highland Railway, but retained running powers for his rolling stock over the lines of what became the London, Midland and Scottish Railway until the nationalisation of the British Railway system after the Second World War. One of the finely-appointed saloons built for the family in 1899 became the prototype for the Royal rolling stock in use between 1903 and 1941. The station at Dunrobin was closed at the time of the Beeching cuts of 1963, as was the branch line from the Mound ot Dornoch, but Dunrobin was re-opened in 1985 as part of a drive to encourage tourists. From Helmsdale, the railway cut inland through the strath of Kildonan via Altnabreac to Georgemas, from which branch lines ran to Wick and Thurso, the termini being reached in 1874.

The Invershin Rail Viaduct, Sutherland, crossing the Kyle of Sutherland involved the construction of five arches with a total girder span of around 230 feet. It formed a part of the Sutherland Railway which operated as far as Golspie by 1868. In 1871 a platform was opened at the Culrain (southern) end of the viaduct initially as a request stop, and two years later, a conventional one. By 1871, the Highland Railway had taken over operations from the Sutherland Railway, including that section north of Golspie previously operated as a private railway by the Duke of Sutherland. As the distance between Culrain and Invershin Station at opposite ends of the viaduct was less than a quarter of a mile and there was no nearby road crossing, until 1917 it was possible to purchase a third class ticket for the journey between these stations at a cost of ½d, the lowest fare in the Highland Railway system, and presumably one of the shortest scheduled railway journeys in the United Kingdom. The railway viaduct also provided a crossing for the telegraph wires. The telegraph reached Caithness in 1868.

Helmsdale Station from the west. The extension northwards of the railway beyond Golspie was initially undertaken privately by the Duke of Sutherland following the Act of 1870. It was intended to service parts of the Sutherland Estates. Because of severe engineering problems, initially the line ran only from a temporary station at Dunrobin to just south of Helmsdale, the track being physically separated from the Sutherland Railway. A temporary station at Gartymore, West Helmsdale, opened in autumn of 1870 permitted a private service between there and Dunrobin. As the Act permitting the line to be built was only passed in June of that year, it must be presumed that construction had started well in advance of parliamentary sanction. Helmsdale station was opened in 1871, and the Highland Railway took over operation from 19th June of that year. The photograph gives an impression of the engine sheds and station at Helmsdale. A down train with four carriages can be seen at the station. The carriages appear to be four-wheeled 'ribbon' carriages of a fairly early design, suggesting that the train was the Duke of Sutherland's, for the family retained the right to operate on the system. The croft strips run down towards the station with cornstooks, haycoles and crops of potatoes much in evidence. The ruins of Helmsdale Castle can be seen on the extreme right, overlooking the harbour.

Dunrobin Station, Sutherland, was opened in 1870 as a private station for the Duke's private railway which ran from Dunrobin to Helmsdale. In that year it really functioned as a temporary terminus. In the following year the system was connected with the Sutherland Railway, and almost immediately taken over by the Highland Railway, when Dunrobin Station reverted to its private status as a place where trains halted by request to serve Dunrobin Castle, a short drive down the avenue. The original station building shown in this photograph was reconstructed in 1902. The porter's barrow proudly bears the insignia 'Duke of Sutherland' on it shafts, while the waiting room is thoughtfully provided with a stove, as shown by the chimney at the rear. After many years of closure, the station at Dunrobin re-opened as a request stop in 1985.

This view of Thurso from the railway includes the new bridge (1887), the railway station (1874, for Caithness and Sutherland Railway), and Thurso Castle (1872). The Mall (1894) alongside Janet Street is shown in an apparently uncared-for state, suggesting that the photograph may have been taken in the early 1890's. The small reservoir at the back of the floodplain in the right middle distance originally provided water for the cornmill. The tall brick chimneys of the flagstone pavement works are still a feature of the riverbank downstream of the bridge.

Buildings and Monuments

The trim estate buildings at the foot of Berriedale Braes catches the photographer's eye.

The Tongue Hotel, Sutherland, with Ben Loyal in the background.

The splendidly ornate Culag Hotel, Lochinver, with two maids taking the sea air at the main entrance.

The Lairg Hotel with coach and horses about to depart with three passengers.

The farm buildings at Ackergill, Wick, display the architectural qualities of the flagstones, although the brick chimney introduces a slightly alien material to the Caithness scene. Note the supplies of peat for power.

The Schoolhouse, Lochinver, Sutherland.

The Memorial Fountain, Golspie.

The monument to Robert Dick, Thurso. Robert Dick owned a bakehouse in Wilson's Lane, Thurso, during the middle decades of the 19th century. In his spare time, Dick studied and recorded many aspects of the natural environment, notably botany, entomology and geology. He carefully recorded, collected and preserved much of his material. Many of the geological specimens were forwarded to Hugh Miller, the Cromarty stone mason and geologist. The obelisk to his memory shown here stands in Thurso Cemetery (cemetery opened 1872).

Scrabster (Holborn Head) Lighthouse (1862) was designed by David and Thomas Stevenson. The schooners lying in Scarbster Roads appear to be riding low, suggesting that they are waiting for suitable high tides to enter Thurso harbour. Sheepskins are apparently drying within the lighthouse enclosure beside the sun dial.

Cape Wrath Lighthouse was established in 1828. The engineer was Robert Stevenson. The name of this most north-westerly point on the Scottish mainland is said to derive from a Norse word meaning 'turning place'. Although on the mainland, because of its remoteness, Cape Wrath has always been classed as 'rock station', that is one unsuitable for wives and children. It is therefore probable that the three ladies present were day visitors from the Kyle of Durness ferry.

Villages

Dunbeath, Caithness. The smithy and carpentry occupies a prominent part of this view of Dunbeath. The yard contains wheels, wagons, carriages as well as timber planks in various lengths. The mill, mill lade and hotel also feature in the photograph. The old quarries in the far bank of the river are abandoned and colonised by birch scrub. The crops and hay coles in the background indicate a mid-summer scene.

Lairg, from the manse, with the hotel partly concealed by the trees near the loch side. In this view, the line of the main street is scarcely developed.

In this view of Lairg from the east, the line of the main street can be picked out. The village school is on the right and Lairg Lodge on the middle skyline.